Bankruptcy's Effect on Product Identification in Asbestos Personal Injury Cases

Lloyd Dixon and Geoffrey McGovern

For more information on this publication, visit www.rand.org/t/rr907

Library of Congress Cataloging-in-Publication Data is available for this
publication.
ISBN: 978-0-8330-9018-8

Published by the RAND Corporation, Santa Monica, Calif.
© Copyright 2015 RAND Corporation
RAND® is a registered trademark.

Cover image via sakura/Fotolia.

Support RAND
Make a tax-deductible charitable contribution at
www.rand.org/giving/contribute

www.rand.org

Preface

In the past 15 years, payments by asbestos bankruptcy trusts have played an increasingly important role in compensating asbestos injuries and have become a matter of contention between plaintiffs' and defendants' attorneys. Plaintiffs now often receive compensation both from the trusts and through a tort case. At issue is how this multisource compensation system affects the payments by defendants that remain solvent and total plaintiff compensation. What outcomes occur depend fundamentally on whether evidence of exposure to the products of the bankrupt parties is introduced in the tort case. The remaining solvent defendants could end up paying more than when such evidence is not developed than when it is developed. Similarly, plaintiffs could receive more compensation when such evidence is not developed than when it is.

This report examines the extent to which exposures to a firm's asbestos-containing products cease to be identified once the firm declares bankruptcy. It also summarizes differing perspectives on whether the findings are a cause for concern.

This report is part of a larger research project on asbestos bankruptcy trusts. An initial report provides an overview of the trusts and compiles publicly available information on the assets, outlays, claim-approval criteria, and governing boards of the leading trusts.[1] A subsequent report examines how the establishment of trusts potentially

---

[1] Lloyd Dixon, Geoffrey McGovern, and Amy Coombe, *Asbestos Bankruptcy Trusts: An Overview of Trust Structure and Activity with Detailed Reports on the Largest Trusts*, Santa Monica, Calif.: RAND Corporation, TR-872-ICJ, 2010.

affects total plaintiff compensation and payments by defendants that remain solvent.[2]

This research was supported by the RAND Institute for Civil Justice (ICJ) and by contributions from the following asbestos defendants and organizations: Ampco-Pittsburgh Corporation; CertainTeed Corporation; Coalition for Litigation Justice; Crane Company; Dow Chemical Company; E. I. du Pont de Nemours and Company; EnPro Industries; General Electric Company; Georgia-Pacific Corporation; Owens-Illinois, Inc.; and the U.S. Chamber Institute for Legal Reform. Three other asbestos defendants who chose not to be identified also sponsored the study. The views expressed in this report are those of the authors and do not necessarily reflect those of the research sponsors.

The RAND Institute for Civil Justice

The ICJ is dedicated to improving the civil justice system by supplying policymakers and the public with rigorous and nonpartisan research. Its studies identify trends in litigation and inform policy choices concerning liability, compensation, regulation, risk management, and insurance. The institute builds on a long tradition of RAND Corporation research characterized by an interdisciplinary, empirical approach to public policy issues and rigorous standards of quality, objectivity, and independence.

ICJ research is supported by pooled grants from a range of sources, including corporations, trade and professional associations, individuals, government agencies, and private foundations. All its reports are subject to peer review and disseminated widely to policymakers, practitioners in law and business, other researchers, and the public.

The ICJ is part of RAND Justice, Infrastructure, and Environment, a division of the RAND Corporation dedicated to improving policy and decisionmaking in a wide range of policy domains, including civil and criminal justice, infrastructure protection and homeland

---

[2] Lloyd Dixon and Geoffrey McGovern, *Asbestos Bankruptcy Trusts and Tort Compensation*, Santa Monica, Calif.: RAND Corporation, MG-1104-ICJ, 2011.

security, transportation and energy policy, and environmental and natural resources policy.

Questions or comments about this report should be sent to the project leader, Lloyd Dixon (Lloyd_Dixon@rand.org). For more information on the Institute for Civil Justice, see http://www.rand.org/icj or contact the director (icjdirector@rand.org).

Contents

Preface iii
Figures and Tables ix
Summary xi
Acknowledgments xvii
Abbreviations xix

CHAPTER ONE
Introduction and Background on Asbestos Bankruptcies 1
The Importance of Evidence of Exposures to the Products of Bankrupt
    Parties 3
Previous Investigations of Bankruptcy's Effect on Product
    Identification 8

CHAPTER TWO
Data Used to Assess Bankruptcy's Impact on Product
    Identification 13
Case Selection 13
Collection of Case Documents 16
Coding of Case Documents 21
Firm Selection 23
Definition of Product-Identification Rates 23

CHAPTER THREE

Findings 25
Bankruptcy's Effect on What Products Are Identified in
    Interrogatories 25
Findings When We Include the Products Identified in Depositions........ 32

CHAPTER FOUR

Discussion 37

APPENDIXES

A. **Firms Whose Product Identification We Analyzed** 41
B. **Alternative Approaches for Estimating Bankruptcy's Effect
    on Product Identification** 45

References 51

Figures and Tables

Figures

S.1. Frequency of Product Identification in Interrogatories After Bankruptcy xiii

S.2. Product Identification Before and After Bankruptcy in Cases with Both Interrogatories and Depositions xiv

Tables

1.1. Bankruptcy's Potential Effects on Plaintiff Compensation and Payments by Remaining Solvent Defendants 6

2.1. Number of Bankruptcies and Cases in the Sample, by Year Filed 19

2.2. Characteristics of Plaintiffs in the Sampled Cases 20

2.3. Number of Cases for Which Different Document Types Were Coded 22

3.1. Product-Identification Rate Pre- and Postbankruptcy Based on Interrogatory Responses 26

3.2. Logistic Regression Analysis of Bankruptcy's Effect on Product Identification in Interrogatories 29

3.3. Illustration of Change in Product-Identification Rates Postbankruptcy 30

3.4. Product-Identification Rate Pre- and Postbankruptcy for Cases with Both Interrogatories and Depositions 33

3.5. Logistic Regression Analysis of Bankruptcy's Effects on Product Identification in Interrogatories and Depositions 34

3.6.   Product-Identification Responses in Interrogatories and
       Depositions for Cases with Both Interrogatories and
       Depositions... 35
A.1.   Firms Whose Product Identification We Analyzed.............. 41
B.1.   Linear Regression Analysis of Bankruptcy's Effect on
       Product Identification in Interrogatories......................... 45
B.2.   Logistic Regression Analysis of Bankruptcy's Average
       Effect on Product Identification................................. 48

Summary

One of the most significant developments in asbestos litigation in the past 15 years is the rising rate of bankruptcy among asbestos defendants. More than 100 companies have filed for bankruptcy at least in part because of asbestos lawsuits. As a result, contemporary asbestos litigation now involves both tort suits against solvent defendants and claims for compensation filed with the specially created asbestos bankruptcy trusts. This report analyzes the interaction between these two compensation systems. The analysis provides empirical evidence that bankruptcy reduces the likelihood that exposure to the asbestos-containing products of the bankrupt parties will be identified in the interrogatories and depositions in subsequent tort cases. The absence of information on such products complicates the determination of compensation for plaintiffs and payments by solvent defendants.

The outcome of an asbestos lawsuit crucially depends on whether evidence of exposure to the products of bankrupt parties is introduced in the tort case. If it is not, then all fault can be assigned to the remaining solvent defendants. These defendants are likely to end up paying more when such evidence is not developed than when it is. Plaintiffs might receive more in compensation from the courts and trusts combined if fault is not allocated to the bankrupt parties.

To empirically address this issue, we examined how often the products of 43 firms that went bankrupt between 1998 and 2010 were identified in mesothelioma cases brought by two sets of plaintiffs with similar exposure histories: 47 plaintiffs who worked at the

Brooklyn Naval Shipyard (BNS)[1] in New York between 1940 and 1949 and 39 plaintiffs who joined the Navy between 1950 and 1954 and were stationed at West Coast bases or on ships that were serviced on the West Coast (to which we refer collectively as West Coast Navy, or WCN, cases).[2]

We compared the rate at which plaintiffs identified exposure to a firm's products before and after the firm's bankruptcy. To determine the rate of identification, we looked at both interrogatories and depositions that occurred during the litigation. Answers to the interrogatories examined in our study were completed in writing by plaintiffs' lawyers and paraprofessionals and typically were submitted early in the case. Depositions usually occur later in the process, with questions asked by the defense attorneys and answered in person by the plaintiff, family members, or coworkers.

Plaintiffs' Exposure to the Asbestos-Containing Products of a Bankrupt Firm Is Identified Less Frequently After Bankruptcy Than Before

Results from the review of interrogatories alone (shown in Figure S.1) indicate that the longer the time between a firm's bankruptcy and the date a tort case is filed, the lower the likelihood that the bankrupt firm's products will be identified in the tort case. For BNS cases, a prebankruptcy identification rate of 20 percent falls to very low levels—4 percent—for cases filed two years or more after the bankruptcy of the firm.[3]

---

[1] The database we used uses the name *Brooklyn Naval Shipyard* for the U.S. Navy Yard, New York, in Brooklyn.

[2] We looked at asbestos tort filings for 1998 through 2010. We looked at bankruptcy filings for 1995 through 2010. We went back to 1998 for tort filings because locating interrogatories and depositions for cases filed before that was too onerous. We chose 1995 for bankruptcy filings to allow us to investigate a lag between when a firm files for bankruptcy and the effect on the product exposures identified in the case.

[3] Throughout this report, *bankruptcy* refers to the date on which a firm files for bankruptcy.

Figure S.1
Frequency of Product Identification in Interrogatories After Bankruptcy

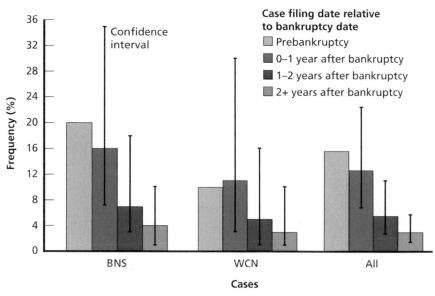

RAND *RR907-S.1*

The prebankruptcy identification rate is lower for the WCN cases, but that rate also declines substantially the more time has passed since bankruptcy. As shown by the 95-percent confidence interval for the WCN cases, there is considerable uncertainty in the estimates.[4] A conclusion that bankruptcy reduces the identification rate for WCN cases should thus be viewed as tentative. A larger sample of cases would increase the precision of the estimates.

The right-most set of columns shows the average effect of the two sets of cases combined. The smaller confidence intervals (that is, greater accuracy) are a consequence of the larger sample size.

These findings cannot automatically be extrapolated to other states with different liability regimes, to states with different requirements for showing that exposure contributes to injury, or to cases with other exposure histories in which maritime law does not apply.

---

[4]   The true underlying identification rate falls within this range with 95-percent probability.

An Increase in Product Identification in Depositions Does Not Offset a Decline in Product Identification in Interrogatories

If the number of products that plaintiffs identify in interrogatories declines after bankruptcy, one might expect additional products to be identified during depositions. Examining cases for which both interrogatories and depositions were available, we tallied whether products from any of the 43 firms included in the study were identified in either type of document and, if they were, whether the exposure was affirmed or denied or whether plaintiffs were unsure about whether they were exposed.

As Figure S.2 shows, fewer firms were identified in interrogatories and depositions combined postbankruptcy than prebankruptcy, and there is no indication of a rise in the frequency with which plain-

Figure S.2
Product Identification Before and After Bankruptcy in Cases with Both Interrogatories and Depositions

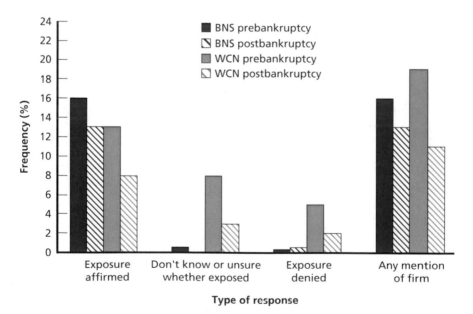

tiffs either denied or were unsure about exposure. The implication is that, during depositions, defendants do little to counter the decline in the number of firms identified in interrogatories, such as by exploring exposures to bankrupt parties not identified in interrogatories.

Views Are Sharply Divided About Whether These Findings Are a Cause for Concern

Are these findings a cause for concern? Among the attorneys we interviewed or who commented on interim findings, plaintiffs' and defendants' attorneys gave different answers to this question. Plaintiffs' attorneys said that the system is working. Some plaintiffs' attorneys believe that it is appropriate for them to focus on the solvent defendants because doing so furthers their clients' interests by maximizing the compensation they could receive for the harms they suffered. Because solvent defendants are the only ones available to be sued, plaintiffs' attorneys remarked that pursuing liability claims against those firms is both logical and appropriate. Some plaintiffs' attorneys further noted that defendants have many options when it comes to investigating and introducing potential exposures to bankrupt defendants' products: They can explore exposures to bankrupt firms during depositions, or they can introduce ship logs and other information on work history to establish exposure. The information about insolvent defendants' products, plaintiffs contend, is widely known and available for introduction—by the defense—as part of the defense's litigation strategy if it so chooses. Responding to preliminary findings of our study, plaintiffs' attorneys point out that, even though product-identification rates in interrogatories and depositions decline, all exposures could end up being identified if the case proceeds to verdict. If a case settles before verdict, those settlements are voluntary on the defense's part.

Defendants and defense attorneys, on the other hand, list a variety of factors that discourage them from probing exposures to bankrupt parties' products during deposition and point out that, even though defense attorneys can hire experts to prove that a plaintiff was exposed to the product of a bankrupt party, doing so is much more expensive and less persuasive than a plaintiff's acknowledgment of exposure to such products. It is the defense attorneys' view that case-management orders require plaintiffs to identify, during pretrial discovery, *all* exposures to asbestos-containing products, not just the products of the solvent companies they are pursing in litigation. Consequently, they believe that a falling rate of product identification postbankruptcy is of major concern. Defendants and defense attorneys argue for expanding and better enforcing requirements that trust claims be filed before trial. They also support modifying case-management orders to clarify that plaintiffs must disclose, in interrogatory responses, all exposures to asbestos-containing products, regardless of whether the product was produced by a currently bankrupt firm.

This report does not take a position in this debate but offers empirical evidence that should help elected officials, judges, and lawyers decide whether the issue merits a policy response.

Acknowledgments

The study reported here would not have been possible without the participation of the many asbestos defendants that collected complaints, interrogatories, and depositions for the selected cases. These documents were not always readily available, and these firms often went to considerable lengths to locate them. We thank them for their efforts.

We are also indebted to Marc Scarcella and Peter Kelso at Bates White for the information and advice they shared during the course of the project. They shared their experiences extracting product exposures from case documents and helped us identify linkages between subsidiaries and successor firms.

Detailed and insightful peer reviews were provided by S. Todd Brown at the State University of New York at Buffalo Law School and Michael Dworsky at RAND. We also received very helpful comments on interim drafts from 14 informed stakeholders. The perspectives of defendants, plaintiffs, and academics were represented. Several chose to remain anonymous; so as not to selectively identify those who provided comments, we are keeping the identities of all commenters confidential. At RAND, we thank Paul Heaton for the advice he provided during the course of the project and Jamie Morikawa for leading the fundraising effort and updating sponsors during the course of the project. Lisa Bernard skillfully edited the document.

Abbreviations

BNS   Brooklyn Naval Shipyard

WCN   West Coast Navy

CHAPTER ONE

Introduction and Background on Asbestos Bankruptcies

Exposure to asbestos, once widely used in industrial and consumer products, can result in asbestosis and mesothelioma, a cancer that is inevitably fatal.[1] As a consequence, companies that produced or used asbestos and asbestos-containing products faced enormous liability. Asbestos litigation began in earnest in the 1970s and continues to this day, the longest-running mass tort in U.S. history.[2] One of the most significant developments in asbestos litigation in the past 15 years involves the scores of asbestos defendants that have filed for bankruptcy because of the large volume of lawsuits and their expected liability. As a result of these bankruptcies, compensation for injuries caused by asbestos

---

[1] According to the National Library of Medicine of the National Institutes of Health, average survival time for a patient with malignant mesothelioma ranges from four to 18 months, depending on the stage of the tumor, the patient's age and general health, whether surgery is an option, and the patient's response to treatment:

> There is usually no cure, unless the disease is found extremely early and the tumor can be completely removed with surgery. Most of the time when the disease is diagnosed it is too advanced for surgery. Chemotherapy or radiation may be used to reduce symptoms. Combining certain chemotherapy drugs may help decrease symptoms, but it will not cure the cancer. ("Mesothelioma: Malignant," MedlinePlus, updated May 29, 2014)

[2] Stephen J. Carroll, Deborah R. Hensler, Jennifer Gross, Elizabeth M. Sloss, Matthias Schonlau, Allan Abrahamse, and J. Scott Ashwood, *Asbestos Litigation*, Santa Monica, Calif.: RAND Corporation, MG-162-ICJ, 2005.

now involves both regular tort suits and claims filed with specially created asbestos bankruptcy trusts.[3]

How the two systems interact is a hotly debated topic. Our previous research has explored how the bankruptcies can affect the total amount a plaintiff can recover from trusts and the tort case combined and the amount paid by defendants that remain solvent.[4] The outcomes depend fundamentally on whether evidence of exposure to the products of the bankrupt parties is introduced in the tort case. The remaining solvent defendants could end up paying more when such evidence is not developed than when it is developed. Similarly, plaintiffs could receive more when such evidence is not developed than when it is.

This report examines the extent to which exposures to a firm's asbestos-containing products cease to be identified in tort cases once the firm declares bankruptcy. It examines changes caused by bankruptcy in the nature of the exposure information provided in plaintiffs' responses to interrogatories and in depositions of plaintiffs and plaintiffs' family members and coworkers. As we discuss below, additional exposure information could be introduced after the interrogatories and depositions, but a change in the information provided in interrogatories and depositions signals a change in plaintiff, and possibly defendant, behavior versus what would have happened without bankruptcy. This report explores possible explanations for the observed change in product identification and examines the significance of the findings for asbestos litigation.

In the remainder of this introductory section, we summarize how the structural linkages between the tort and trust systems affect incentives to identify the asbestos-containing products of bankrupt firms in tort cases. We also summarize bankruptcy's effect on product identification in asbestos cases. Then, in Chapter Two, we describe this study's methodology for examining product-identification trends pre-

---

[3]   For a recent overview of asbestos litigation, see Georgene Vairo, "Lessons Learned by the Reporter: Is Disaggregation the Answer to the Asbestos Mess?" *Tulane Law Review*, Vol. 88, No. 6, 2014, pp. 1039–1044.

[4]   See Lloyd Dixon and Geoffrey McGovern, *Asbestos Bankruptcy Trusts and Tort Compensation*, Santa Monica, Calif.: RAND Corporation, MG-1104-ICJ, 2011.

and postbankruptcy. Chapter Three presents the results of the analysis, and Chapter Four discusses the significance of the findings.

The Importance of Evidence of Exposures to the Products of Bankrupt Parties

The high volume of cases brought against asbestos manufacturers beginning in the 1970s and large payouts encouraged scores of companies to seek novel ways to manage their asbestos liabilities. The main innovation was the establishment of special asbestos bankruptcy trusts created pursuant to Section 524(g) of the Bankruptcy Code.[5] As part of the reorganization plan, a company provides substantial funding for a trust (including stock, insurance recoveries, and cash) and, in exchange, is shielded from the predecessor company's asbestos liabilities. A channeling injunction diverts all current and future claims arising from asbestos exposure to the trust rather than the company. The trust provides compensation via court-approved distribution rules for current and future claims.[6] In short, the bankruptcy-trust approach allows companies to shed their asbestos liabilities, to reorganize as viable businesses, and to establish funds to compensate current and future claimants.

Trusts are typically not funded at levels that allow full payment of the estimated amount the plaintiff would have received had the defendant remained solvent. Each trust sets a payment percentage that is used to determine the actual payment a claimant will be offered. A review of 26 of the largest trusts puts the median payment percentage at 25 percent, with the range running from 1.1 percent to 100 percent.[7] Thus, a plaintiff can receive less from a trust than if he or she had sued

---

[5]   U.S. Code, Title 11, Bankruptcy, Chapter 5, Creditors, the debtor, and the estate, Subchapter II, Debtor's duties and benefits, Section 524, Effect of discharge.

[6]   See Lloyd Dixon, Geoffrey McGovern, and Amy Coombe, *Asbestos Bankruptcy Trusts: An Overview of Trust Structure and Activity with Detailed Reports on the Largest Trusts*, Santa Monica, Calif.: RAND Corporation, TR-872-ICJ, 2010.

[7]   Dixon, McGovern, and Coombe, 2010, p. xv.

the predecessor company prior to its bankruptcy. However, we learned during our interviews that defendants sometimes argue that the payment percentage is applied to an estimated claim value that exceeds what the plaintiff would have received had the firm remained solvent and thus that the net effect on plaintiff compensation is not always clear.

The advent of trusts as a mechanism for managing asbestos liabilities has fundamentally altered the course of asbestos litigation. At a basic level, asbestos litigation has changed because now more than 100 companies have claimed the protections of Chapter 11 of the Bankruptcy Code in part because of their asbestos liabilities.[8] These companies, many of which were the major producers of asbestos-containing products, are no longer subject to lawsuits. Hence, there are both bankrupt parties whose putative share of liability is now represented by the trust funds (which held assets in excess of $18 billion as of 2012)[9] and solvent defendants that are facing lawsuits for asbestos-related injuries.

The fact that there are now bankruptcy trusts and solvent defendants has complicated the business of establishing liabilities and calculating the appropriate compensation due deserving plaintiffs in the tort system. Whereas all claims for compensation were once managed in the tort system, a parallel system of compensation now exists through the trusts. This parallelism has raised concerns among current asbestos defendants that all exposures will not be considered in determining the responsibility of the remaining solvent defendants and that plaintiffs could receive more than they would have had the firms not declared bankruptcy.

Our previous research examined the linkages between the tort system and asbestos bankruptcy trusts.[10] We found a great deal of vari-

---

[8]   Crowell and Moring, "Chart 1: Company Name and Year of Bankruptcy Filing (Chronologically)," 2660535, revised September 19, 2014.

[9]   Marc C. Scarcella and Peter R. Kelso, "Asbestos Bankruptcy Trusts: A 2013 Overview of Trust Assets, Compensation and Governance," *Mealey's Asbestos Bankruptcy Report*, Vol. 12, No. 11, June 2013, p. 35.

[10] Four potential linkages were examined: the information linkage, the setoff linkage, the indirect-claim linkage, and the trust payment–limitation linkage (Dixon and McGovern, 2011, p. xii).

ation across states with regard to how trust compensation enters into the determination of tort awards, with the variation caused by

- differences in liability standards and rules on when trust claims must be filed during a tort case
- whether setoffs for trust payments are allowed in determining tort awards
- whether fault can be assigned to bankrupt parties.

Informed by our analysis of these linkages, we identified the potential effects of bankruptcy on plaintiff compensation from trusts and tort combined. We also identified the effects of bankruptcy on the payments by defendants that remain solvent.

Table 1.1 summarizes findings from our previous work on the potential differences in compensation received by the same plaintiff if (1) the tort case were filed before any parties had declared bankruptcy and (2) the case were filed after some parties had declared bankruptcy and set up trusts.[11] It also reports differences in payments by parties that remain solvent. As can be seen, the outcomes depend significantly on whether evidence of exposures to the products of bankrupt parties is developed in the tort case.

In states with joint and several liability, one would expect the compensation received by plaintiffs from trusts and tort combined to remain unchanged whether or not evidence about exposure to bankrupt parties' products is developed.[12] Because, under joint and sev-

---

[11] Although the vast majority of asbestos cases settle, the settlements are guided by expected outcomes at trial, taking into account legal, expert, and other costs associated with going to trial. For a detailed discussion of how bankruptcy can affect outcomes of plaintiffs and remaining solvent defendants, see Dixon and McGovern, 2011.

[12] Joint-and-several-liability doctrine holds each individual defendant liable for the full damages; the onus is then placed on the defendant to seek contribution from the other responsible parties. In contrast, several-liability doctrine is a legal rule that limits a defendant's liability for a harm to the portion of the harm that the defendant caused. If, for example, three defendants each contributed 33 percent of the fault for an injury, a several-liability jurisdiction would hold each defendant responsible for one-third of the damages. Recently, some states have shifted away from the traditional joint-and-several-liability rule. For a discussion of the various liability regimes, see Robert S. Peck, "The Development of the Law of

Table 1.1
Bankruptcy's Potential Effects on Plaintiff Compensation and Payments by Remaining Solvent Defendants

Outcome	Bankruptcy's Effect on Outcome If Evidence of Exposure to Products of Bankrupt Parties Is or Is Not Developed	
	Is Developed	Is Not Developed
State with joint and several liability		
Plaintiff compensation from trusts and tort combined	Unchanged	Unchanged
Payments by remaining solvent defendants	Increase	Increase by more than when exposure is developed[a]
State with several liability		
Plaintiff compensation from trusts and tort combined	Can decrease	Can increase
Payments by remaining solvent defendants	Remain unchanged	Increase

SOURCE: Based on Dixon and McGovern, 2011.

[a] Or, put another way, payments by remaining solvent defendants increase more than when the evidence is developed.

eral liability, a single liable defendant is responsible for compensating 100 percent of a plaintiff's injuries, it makes no difference whether there is evidence of exposure to a bankrupt party's products. If such evidence of exposures is developed, one would expect any payments by remaining solvent defendants to increase by the amount of the bankrupt firms' pre-reorganization liability that the trust does not cover.[13] Such an increase would be consistent with the intent of joint and sev-

---

Joint and Several Liability," *Federation of Defense and Corporate Counsel Quarterly*, Vol. 55, No. 4, Summer 2005, pp. 469–478.

[13] A defendant that pays the full judgment in a joint-and-several-liability jurisdiction gains the right to pursue trust claims. As discussed earlier in this section, trusts apply a payment percentage that creates a wedge between the trust payment and what would have been the value of the claim had the predecessor firm remained solvent. The paying defendant could thus end up covering the difference between the claim value and the amount paid by the trust.

eral liability. However, when exposure to the product of a bankrupt party is not developed in the tort case, any remaining solvent defendants would not have the information needed to take advantage of resources available from the trusts and thus would pay more than if all product exposures were identified.[14]

The potential outcomes are quite different in several-liability states. If information is developed on the exposure to the products of the bankrupt parties when the case is filed postbankruptcy, plaintiff compensation from trust and tort combined can decrease. Such an outcome would occur to the extent that the trust does not cover a bankrupt firm's prebankruptcy liability. Payments by remaining solvent defendants would remain unchanged. In contrast, if evidence of exposure to a product of a bankrupt party were not developed, both plaintiff compensation and payments by the remaining solvent defendants could increase. Plaintiff compensation would increase if, for example, all fault were assigned to the remaining solvent defendants at trial and the plaintiff then recovered additional amounts from the trusts. The remaining solvent defendants would pay more because fault was not appropriately allocated to the bankrupt parties.

Plaintiffs therefore have disincentives to develop evidence of exposure to the product of a bankrupt party. Failure to develop such evidence can increase the likelihood that at least one of the remaining solvent defendants will be found liable.[15] Also, in several-liability states, less exposure to the products of bankrupt parties can mean that more fault is assigned to and larger payment received from the remaining solvent defendants.

---

[14] Now, instead of just covering the difference between the claim value and the trust payment, the paying defendant covers the entire claim value.

[15] Exposure to an asbestos-containing product does not automatically result in the product's producer being held liable. As discussed in Chapter Two, asbestos cases can be subject to maritime law. For a defendant to be found liable under maritime law, the plaintiff must show that the relevant products were a substantial contributing factor in causing the injury. Some defendants with whose representatives we spoke during the course of this study argue that reducing the number of other exposures identified in the case can increase the likelihood that the products of the remaining parties will be found to have substantially contributed to the injury.

In contrast to the disincentives that plaintiffs have, remaining solvent defendants have incentives to develop evidence of exposure to the products of bankrupt parties. Traditionally, in tort, each side develops its own evidence of causes of the injury.

As pointed out in our previous work, there is a great deal of dispute between plaintiffs' and defense attorneys in asbestos cases about who is responsible for developing evidence of the products and practices of bankrupt firms. Plaintiffs' attorneys argue that defense attorneys can use discovery tools to uncover exposure information and that, in many cases, both parties already know the likely exposures even before the case begins because of other cases from the same workplace. Defense attorneys respond that plaintiffs' attorneys can influence which exposures plaintiffs recall during the case proceedings and that, without plaintiff cooperation, it is much more expensive to establish exposure and the result much less persuasive to a jury. It is important to note, however, that, regardless of who is to blame, a plaintiff's failure to identify exposure to the product of a bankrupt party or a defendant's failure to develop exposure evidence can alter the outcomes for both plaintiffs and defendants.

Previous Investigations of Bankruptcy's Effect on Product Identification

Previous investigations provide initial evidence that exposure to a product of a bankrupt party is identified less frequently postbankruptcy than prebankruptcy. In a recent bankruptcy case estimating the asbestos liabilities of Garlock Sealing Technologies,[16] Judge George Hodges found "substantial evidence" of efforts by some plaintiffs' firms to "withhold evidence of exposure to other asbestos products and to delay filing claims against bankrupt defendants' asbestos trusts until obtaining recoveries from Garlock (and other viable defendants)."[17] These conclusions were based on numerous types of evidence, includ-

---

[16] Garlock is a company that has made gaskets that contained asbestos.

[17] *In re Garlock Sealing Techs., LLC*, 2014 Bankr. LEXIS 155, January 10, 2014, p. 30.

ing deposition of lawyers involved in the litigation and 220 high-value cases in which plaintiffs' discovery responses conflicted with information provided to bankruptcy trusts or with voting in bankruptcy cases.[18] Judge Hodges permitted Garlock to have full discovery in 15 of the 220 cases. In summarizing evidence of misrepresentations he found "surprising and persuasive," Judge Hodges concluded that

> Garlock demonstrated that exposure evidence was withheld in *each and every one* of [the 15 cases.] The discovery in this proceeding showed that what had been withheld in the tort cases— on average plaintiffs disclosed about 2 exposures to bankruptcy companies' products, but after settling with Garlock made claims against about 19 such companies' Trusts [italics in original].[19]

The court's findings imply that, for these 15 cases, exposures were disclosed for approximately 10 percent of the bankrupt firms to whose products the plaintiff had been exposed.[20] However, these 15 cases are not a random or necessarily a representative sample and might well be the most extreme examples of incomplete disclosure. In addition, plaintiffs' attorneys question the relevance of the findings. They point out that some trusts will pay compensation on the basis of evidence that would be insufficient to establish liability in the tort case. It can thus be appropriate, in their view, to file trust claims while not disclosing the exposures in the tort case.

A study of mesothelioma cases filed in the Court of Common Pleas of Philadelphia County between 1991 and 2010 also provides evidence that product identification declines postbankruptcy.[21] Scarcella,

---

[18] As creditors in the bankruptcy case, plaintiffs are eligible to participate in creditor votes on the reorganization plan. To qualify as a creditor, a plaintiff must allege injury caused by exposure to the bankrupt party's products.

[19] *In re Garlock Sealing Techs.*, 2014, p. 31.

[20] Data on the number of exposures disclosed and not disclosed in the 15 cases are included in the opinion. Thirty-two of a total of 316 total exposures were disclosed. *In re Garlock Sealing Techs.*, 2014, p. 34.

[21] During the period covered by the Scarcella, Kelso, and Cagnoli study (Marc C. Scarcella, Peter R. Kelso, and Joseph Cagnoli, Jr., "The Philadelphia Story: Asbestos Litigation, Bank-

Kelso, and Cagnoli (2012) examined 107 mesothelioma cases and compared the products positively identified in plaintiffs' interrogatory responses and depositions in cases filed before the bankruptcy wave that began in 2000 with cases filed during and after the bankruptcy wave. They found that, prior to the bankruptcy wave, plaintiffs identified approximately eight defendants that produced thermal insulation or refractory products and eventually filed for bankruptcy reorganization. For cases filed between 2006 and 2010 after the bankruptcy wave, approximately four of the now-bankrupt defendants were identified per case, on average.[22] One possible explanation for the findings is that the exposure histories of plaintiffs who filed claims prior to the bankruptcy wave were different from those of plaintiffs who filed after the bankruptcy wave. Scarcella, Kelso, and Cagnoli (2012) presented evidence that the exposure histories of the two groups are similar; however, in their statistical analysis, they did not explicitly control for differences in plaintiff exposure history.

The extent to which exposures to the products of bankrupt parties are identified less frequently postbankruptcy across the litigation as a whole is, as yet, unknown. Judge Hodges believed that "more extensive discovery would show more extensive abuse," and Scarcella, Kelso, and Cagnoli (2012) concluded that it would not be surprising if the findings in Philadelphia were "just as pronounced or even more dramatic in other asbestos dockets across the country."[23] Nonetheless, it is possible that experiences in Philadelphia and in the Garlock case are not common: that the products and litigation history are unrepresentative of the experiences of other asbestos defendants.

To better understand this issue, this report examines how bankruptcy affects product identification in mesothelioma cases filed in two

---

ruptcy Trusts and Changes in Exposure Allegations from 1991–2010," *Mealey's Litigation Report: Asbestos*, Vol. 27, No. 17, October 10, 2012, pp. 1–13), liability for asbestos injuries was joint and several in Pennsylvania. Under a law enacted on June 28, 2011, liability is now several in Pennsylvania, with some exceptions (see Dixon and McGovern, 2011, p. 71).

[22] Scarcella, Kelso, and Cagnoli, 2012, p. 4.

[23] Scarcella, Kelso, and Cagnoli, 2012, p. 12.

other states, California and New York. We explain the methodology in Chapter Two.

CHAPTER TWO

Data Used to Assess Bankruptcy's Impact on Product Identification

The overall concept for the study design was to identify plaintiffs who were similar in terms of asbestos exposure and disease but who differed as to when disease manifested and a tort case filed. Because each case is filed at a different point in time, the firms that are bankrupt at the date of case filing varies across cases, as does the time since each firm's bankruptcy. We used this variation to estimate bankruptcy's effect on product identification. For each case, we reviewed interrogatories and depositions to determine the firms that produced the asbestos-containing products to which the plaintiff indicated exposure. We then estimated the relationship between the frequency with which a firm was identified and the time since bankruptcy. A decline in the frequency as the time since bankruptcy increased would suggest that, once a firm files for bankruptcy, exposures to that firm's product are less likely to be identified in the tort process over time.

The remainder of this chapter begins with a description of the process used to select the cases in the study. Then we discuss the procedures used to collect and code the relevant case documents. Finally, we describe the firms used to examine changes in product identification pre- and postbankruptcy.

Case Selection

We chose two different sets of cases for the study: one consisting of cases filed in California state court and the other consisting of cases filed in New York state court. We chose these two states because they are states with substantial numbers of asbestos filings and because liability is several in some respects.[1] We restricted the analysis to two states first because court rules and procedures vary by state, so bankruptcy's effects on product identification might vary by state. Second, restricting the analysis to two states reduced the time and effort needed to locate the documents needed for the analysis. Litigation in a particular jurisdiction is often handled by local counsel, and restricting the number of different jurisdictions analyzed reduced the number of law firms that we needed to contact for the required documents.

We worked with a large asbestos claim service provider to identify cases with similar exposure histories.[2] To increase the similarity of cases, we included in the study only plaintiffs with mesothelioma. Given available work history, the service provider assigns a primary jobsite to each claim in its database. This is the jobsite at which the majority of asbestos exposure is thought to have occurred. The service provider provided the study team with tabulations of cases by primary jobsite separately for mesothelioma cases filed in California and mesothelioma cases filed in New York.

Given the results, one jobsite in California and one in New York were chosen. Surprisingly, very few primary jobsites had substantial numbers of claims. Because we needed a substantial number of claims for analysis at each jobsite, we had little latitude in selecting the primary jobsites. We selected the primary jobsites with the largest number

---

[1]   We decided to focus on states with several liability because plaintiffs' disincentives to identify the products of bankruptcy parties might be stronger in several-liability states (see the discussion in Chapter One). However, it is important to note that liability in both California and New York is complex and has aspects of both traditional joint and several liability, as well as pure several liability. In California, liability is joint and several for economic damages and several for noneconomic damages. In New York, liability for asbestos injuries is also joint and several for economic damages. If a defendant is found to be 50 percent or less at fault, liability for that defendant will be several for noneconomic damages. However, a defendant in a New York case will be jointly and severally liable for noneconomic damages if that defendant is found to have acted recklessly or to have acted in concert with other parties to conceal the danger of asbestos (Dixon and McGovern, 2011, pp. 62, 67).

[2]   This provider maintains an extensive database of asbestos personal-injury cases.

of claims: the Brooklyn Naval Shipyard (BNS)[3] for claims filed in New York state court and the Puget Sound Naval Shipyard and Intermediate Maintenance Facility in Washington State for claims filed in California courts. It turned out that the common characteristic of exposure in the Puget Sound cases is that the plaintiffs were in the Navy and either were stationed on ships that were serviced on the West Coast of the United States or were stationed at bases on the West Coast. We thus refer to these cases as West Coast Navy (WCN) cases.

The service provider provided work history information for the cases with these primary jobsites. The resources available to the project allowed us to include up to 100 cases in the study, and we selected 100 cases so as to produce two samples, each with similar exposures and each with filing dates that spanned the bankruptcy surge between 2000 and 2002.

Given the work history information for the BNS cases, we restricted our attention to cases in which the plaintiffs worked at BNS between 1940 and 1949. We also restricted cases to those filed in 1998 and later because defendants involved in the litigation indicated that it would be very difficult to obtain interrogatories and depositions for cases filed before 1998. When available, we randomly selected five cases for each filing year between 1998 and 2010, and we selected all available cases for those years in which fewer than five cases were filed.

For WCN, we limited the sample to those plaintiffs who, according to the database, had been at the Puget Sound Naval Shipyard between 1950 and 1964. Again, we selected up to five cases per filing year. We selected a total of 52 BNS and 48 WCN cases.

We selected cases in two different states, each of which had a particular liability regime. The variation in liability regime and causation requirements across states means that results based on these sets of cases cannot necessary be extrapolated to asbestos litigation as a whole. The particular exposure histories of the plaintiffs might also limit relevance of these findings to broader asbestos litigation. Because these cases all involve exposure in and around ships, the causation standard

---

[3] The database we referenced uses the name *Brooklyn Naval Shipyard* for the U.S. Navy Yard, New York, in Brooklyn.

was likely determined by maritime law. Maritime law employs a more stringent causation standard than ordinary tort law does to determine liability. Further work is needed to better understand how the difference in causation standard might affect incentives and party behavior.[4]

Collection of Case Documents

Firms that are defendants in a substantial number of asbestos personal-injury cases were asked to provide the complaints, interrogatories, and depositions for these 100 cases.[5] Both California and New York courts have case-management orders for asbestos cases that include a standard set of interrogatory questions that the plaintiff is required to answer in writing and under oath and to update as more information becomes available.[6] Plaintiffs' lawyers and paraprofessionals who are typically

---

[4]   Maritime law requires a plaintiff raising a product-liability complaint to show that the defendant's product "was a *substantial* factor in causing the injury he suffered" (*Lindstrom v. A-C Prod. Liab. Trust*, 424 F.3d 488 [6th Cir.], September 28, 2005; emphasis added). State tort law relating to product liability might have a lower standard than maritime law's "substantial-factor" test, depending on the theory of liability raised in the complaint and the evidentiary standards for the specific jurisdiction. The substantial-factor aspect of maritime law could provide added disincentives for plaintiffs to identify exposures of bankrupt parties and could render exposures that do not constitute substantial factors irrelevant to liability. Some defendants with whose representatives we spoke during the course of this study argued that the identification of fewer such exposures might increase the chance that solvent defendants will be found liable.

[5]   Most of the defendants were sponsors of this study. Each case was assigned to approximately three of the participating firms, with the assignments based on whether the firm was named in the complaint. Cases for which documents could not be located were subsequently reassigned to other firms. The result was that each participating firm was asked to gather documents on roughly 30 cases. Assigning each case to multiple firms helped increase the likelihood that we would obtain all relevant interrogatories and depositions. There is no court database of all the interrogatories and depositions produced in a case and thus no outside check that we have all the interrogatories and depositions in each of the cases.

[6]   Case-management orders facilitate the development of exposure information. Identifying exposures is complicated by the long elapsed time since the exposure (which often occurred in the 1940s and 1950s for the selected cases) and the fact that, in many cases, the victim is dead and the case filed by the victim's estate. Case-management orders are not necessarily uniform across a state. All the cases in the New York sample were in New York City courts,

very familiar with asbestos-containing products complete the answers, typically early in the case. The New York interrogatory includes questions on the plaintiff's family, medical history, work history, and detailed questions about asbestos exposure. For example, question 16 in the case-management order in effect as of 2001 asks,

> As to each and every employer (including military service) you have had from the time you were first employed to the present, set forth the following:
> Include on the Chart all employers where [sic] you have worked, and all job sites, regardless of whether or not you believe you were exposed to asbestos during the employment. Also, include the source of any product identification information provided on Chart A.[7]

Chart A requires jobsite-specific exposure history and includes columns for the asbestos-containing materials or products that the plaintiff personally used and other asbestos-containing material to which the plaintiff was exposed. For the latter, respondents are asked to identify brand and manufacturer names, if known. The current case-management order for San Francisco superior courts (as of December 2014) requires the plaintiff to list every type of employment (including self-employment) and whether the plaintiff was exposed to asbestos "at this employment" but is not as explicit about identifying brand and manufacturer.[8]

There are differing views of whether these case-management orders direct plaintiffs to disclose all exposures (to the products of bankrupt and solvent firms alike). Defendants argue strongly that the intent of

---

with the same case-management order. The California cases were spread across Alameda, Los Angeles, and San Francisco counties, and the case-management orders differ in each county.

[7] *In re: New York City Asbestos Litigation*, "Defendants' Third Amended Standard Set of Interrogatories and Request for Production of Documents," Appendix C, N.Y. 2001.

[8] For example, see question 26 of Exhibit C of the San Francisco case-management order (*In re Complex Asbestos Litig.*, "Defendants' Standard Interrogatories to Plaintiff (Personal Injury) [Set One]," Super. Ct. California, County of San Francisco, Case CGC-84-828684, November 26, 2013).

these orders is to require disclosure of all exposures. Some plaintiffs' lawyers maintain that the requirements are vague and in flux and that it is unclear whether plaintiffs are required to disclose exposure to the asbestos-containing products of bankrupt companies.

For each case, we requested all interrogatory answers by the plaintiff, including supplemental answers. For convenience, we refer to these documents simply as interrogatories.

Also requested were depositions of the plaintiff, the plaintiff's family and coworkers, and any other depositions related to product identification. We did not request depositions by medical professionals, such as the treating physician, diagnosing physician, B readers,[9] industrial hygienists, and physical therapists, because these depositions typically do not contain product-identification information. Depositions come later in the case than interrogatories and are done under oath and typically in person and transcribed. For the depositions reviewed here, questions were typically asked by defense attorneys and answered by the plaintiff, family members, or coworkers.

The participating firms were able to locate complaints, interrogatories, or depositions for 89 of the 100 cases. After reviewing the interrogatory responses in the 89 cases, we dropped three cases from the study because they did not meet the exposure selection criteria. As can be seen in Table 2.1, some of the cases in the BNS sample were filed before and after the 2000–2002 bankruptcy spike. For the WCN sample, fewer cases were available prior to the bankruptcy spike, but there is still considerable range in the filing dates.

Table 2.2 provides characteristics of plaintiffs in the cases in the sample. The plaintiffs in the WCN sample tend to be born later than those in the BNS sample. Their start dates with the Navy likewise tend to be after the dates the plaintiffs in the BNS sample first began to work at BNS. Reflecting the selection criteria, start dates of the BNS plaintiffs are consistent with working at the BNS for some period between 1940 and 1949. For the WCN sample, the start dates are consistent with the plaintiffs being on West Coast–based ships or West Coast

---

[9]   A B reader is a physician certified by the National Institute for Occupational Safety and Health (NIOSH) to read chest radiographs.

Table 2.1
Number of Bankruptcies and Cases in the Sample, by Year Filed

Year	Bankruptcies Filed[a]	Cases Filed	
		BNS Sample	WCN Sample
Pre-1995	26	0	0
1995	1	0	0
1996	1	0	0
1997	1	0	0
1998	2	3	1
1999	3	5	0
2000	7	5	3
2001	9	5	1
2002	15	4	4
2003	5	5	4
2004	5	4	4
2005	4	4	5
2006	3	5	5
2007	2	5	5
2008	3	1	5
2009	2	1	1
2010	4	0	1
Total 1995–2010	67	47	39
Total all years	93	47	39

[a] Source: Dixon, McGovern, and Coombe, 2010, pp. 47–52.

Navy bases for some period between 1950 and 1964. Consistent with the earlier birth years, the plaintiffs in the BNS sample were older at the time of case filing, and a higher percentage of the plaintiffs had died before the case was filed.

Table 2.2
Characteristics of Plaintiffs in the Sampled Cases

Year	BNS Sample	WCN Sample
Total cases	47	39
Year of birth		
1910–1914	4	0
1915–1919	12	1
1920–1924	17	3
1925–1929	12	0
1930–1934	2	10
1935–1939	0	11
1940–1944	0	11
1945–1949	0	3
Start date at BNS or with the Navy		
1935–1939	4	1
1940–1944	34	1
1945–1949	9	3
1950–1954	0	11
1955–1959	0	11
1960–1964	0	12
Average age at time of case filing (years)[a]	80.3	68.0
Percentage deceased at time of case filing	36	10
Plaintiffs' attorney		
Firm A	29	0
Firm B	9	0
Firm C	6	0
Firm D	0	9
Firm E	0	7

Table 2.2—Continued

Year	BNS Sample	WCN Sample
Firm F	0	5
Firm G	0	5
Other	3	13

[a] For plaintiffs living at the time of case filing.

The two sets of plaintiffs are represented by entirely different sets of plaintiffs' attorneys. As shown in the last set of rows in Table 2.2, each of the seven law firms listed represented plaintiffs who filed in New York state court or California state court, but the firms did not have cases in both jurisdictions. Likewise, the different plaintiffs' firms in the "other" category represent plaintiffs in cases filed in one state or the other, but not both.

Coding of Case Documents

Following coding instructions developed by RAND staff, the claim service provider coded the complaints, interrogatories, and depositions. All firms and product brands named in each document were recorded. Also coded was whether the plaintiff indicated exposure to the product brand or the asbestos-containing products produced by the firm. For each named firm or product brand, coders classified the exposure statements into the following categories:

- affirmative statement of exposure
- explicit denial of exposure
- possible exposure, but discovery continuing
- does not know or is unsure whether there was exposure
- no information provided on whether there was exposure
- claim submitted to the trust of a bankrupt party
- settlement reached with a defendant.

A total of 293 interrogatory and 295 deposition documents were coded. The number of separate depositions coded is likely less than 295 because the same deposition was sometimes split into multiple files. Some duplicate interrogatories and depositions were also likely coded, which would also reduce the number of separate interrogatories and depositions from 293 and 295, respectively.

RAND staff audited a sample of the coded documents. Based on the results of the audit, coding instructions were clarified, and a substantial number of documents were recoded. The recoded documents were audited, and the accuracy of the coding was determined to be sufficient.

The number of cases for which interrogatories and depositions were coded is shown in Table 2.3. As can been seen, interrogatories could be located for 76 of the 86 cases, and depositions could be located for 59. It might not only be that documents that once existed could not be found for some cases. It could also be that a case was settled or dropped before interrogatories were answered or depositions taken. In addition, interrogatories or depositions might not yet have been completed for some of the cases filed toward the end of the study period. The last row of the table reports the number of cases for which both interrogatories and depositions were located. This subset of claims is used in certain analyses.

Table 2.3
Number of Cases for Which Different Document Types Were Coded

Document Type	Cases in the BNS Sample	Cases in the WCN Sample	Total Cases in the Sample
Interrogatory	38	38	76
Deposition	28	31	59
Interrogatory and deposition	19	30	49

Firm Selection

We examined bankruptcy's effect on the probability that the plaintiff indicated exposure to a firm's product for 43 firms that went bankrupt between 1995 and 2010. To allow examination of a lagged response to bankruptcy, we begin this period before the first cases in the sample were filed. As shown in the first column of Table 2.1, 93 firms had declared bankruptcy through 2010. A total of 67 firms declared bankruptcy between 1995 and 2010. However, 22 of these were not referred to in the interrogatories and depositions coded for any of the 86 cases in the analysis. They are thus of limited use in estimating the change in the identification probability attributable to bankruptcy and are not included in the analysis. Also excluded from the analysis are the 26 firms that had filed for bankruptcy prior to 1995. Because these firms were bankrupt during the entire study period (1995 to 2010), they are also of limited use in determining bankruptcy's effects on product identification. We excluded an additional two firms from the analysis because of difficulty identifying the successor firm associated with these companies. Appendix A lists the firms included in the analysis.

Definition of Product-Identification Rates

Combining the number of firms analyzed with the number of cases included in the analysis results in a data set with 3,698 case–firm combinations (86 cases × 43 firms). For each case–firm combination, whether the plaintiff indicated exposure to the firm's products in the case was recorded. We deemed exposure to be indicated when any of the following was true:

- A plaintiff's interrogatory response or a plaintiff's-side deposition contains an affirmative statement of exposure to the firm's products.
- A settlement had been reached with the firm.
- A claim has been submitted to the firm's bankruptcy trust.

We deemed exposure to be indicated if any document reviewed for the case satisfied any of the above criteria.[10] This implies that exposure would be indicated if one deposed party affirmed exposure but another denied it. The identification rate is the proportion of case–firm combinations in which exposure is indicated.

In the next chapter, we examine how the identification rates change following bankruptcy.

---

[10] Including trust submissions as an indicator of exposure might be questioned. Some bankruptcy trusts will pay compensation on the basis of evidence that would be insufficient to establish liability in a tort case. Some thus might argue that trust claims are not always relevant to determining liability in the tort case. In addition, plaintiffs will sometimes submit placeholder claims to trusts in order to meet the limitation period for filing claims. These claims are not yet complete and could, in principle, be withdrawn later if the required exposure evidence cannot be developed. It could thus also be argued that the submission of a trust claim does not necessarily indicate exposure. To acknowledge both of these possible arguments, we also performed the analysis in Chapter Three when submission of a trust claim is not considered to indicate exposure to the predecessor firm's products.

Findings

This chapter reports findings on bankruptcy's impact on product identification. In most cases, we report findings for the BNS and WCS cases separately, although, for some analyses, we combine the two sets of cases. The presentation begins with findings based on the information contained in plaintiffs' responses to the interrogatories. It then considers the additional information provided in depositions of plaintiffs, plaintiffs' families, and plaintiffs' coworkers.

Bankruptcy's Effect on What Products Are Identified in Interrogatories

Table 3.1 reports product-identification rates for the 43 firms that filed for bankruptcy between 1998 and 2010. The first row shows findings for those case–firm combinations in which the case was filed before the firm declared bankruptcy. The second row corresponds to case–firm combinations in which the case was filed within two years following bankruptcy, and the third row reports findings for case–firm combinations in which the case was filed two years or more after the firm's bankruptcy. As can be seen, the identification rate declines as the time between bankruptcy and case filing increases. For the BNS cases, exposure to the firm's products was asserted in 20 percent of the prebankruptcy case–firm combinations. The identification rate drops to 18 percent for cases filed during the first two years following bankruptcy and to 13 percent for those filed two years or more after bankruptcy.

Table 3.1
Product-Identification Rate Pre- and Postbankruptcy Based on
Interrogatory Responses

Case–Firm Combination	BNS Cases[a]		WCN Cases[b]	
	Identification Rate (%)	N	Identification Rate (%)	N
Case filed prebankruptcy	20	735	10	545
Case filed between bankruptcy and two years after bankruptcy	18	249	7	244
Case filed more than two years after bankruptcy	13	650	4	845
All case–firm combinations	17	1,634	7	1,634

NOTE: N refers to number of case–firm combinations.

[a] Based on 1,634 case–firm combinations (38 cases with interrogatories times 43 firms). Five of the 43 firms were not mentioned in any of the interrogatories reviewed for these cases. These five firms might not be relevant to the litigation for these cases. If we excluded these firms, the identification rates would increase.

[b] Based on 1,634 case–firm combinations (38 cases with interrogatories times 43 firms). Twelve of the 43 firms were not mentioned in any of the interrogatories reviewed for these cases. These 12 firms might not be relevant to the litigation for these cases. If we excluded these firms, the identification rates would increase.

The results are similar for the WCN case–firm combinations. The identification rate falls as the time between case filing and bankruptcy increases.[1]

Although illustrative, the tabulations in Table 3.1 are limited. The mix of cases and firms differs pre- and postbankruptcy, creating the possibility that identification-rate differences are due to changes in firm and case mix as opposed to changes in bankruptcy status. Changes in firm and case mix are important because firms vary in terms of the market penetration of their products, which presumably affects the

---

[1] The prebankruptcy identification rate could be lower for the WCN cases than the BCN cases for a variety of reasons. The products produced by the 43 bankrupt firms might just be less relevant to the litigation on the West Coast. Another possible explanation is that, as noted in Chapter Two, the San Francisco case-management order does not explicitly require plaintiffs to identify manufacturer or brand—in contrast to the New York case-management order.

identification rate. In addition, even if plaintiffs have similar exposure histories, their attorneys might differ in strategies for how many exposures to investigate in a claim. As a consequence, pre- and postbankruptcy identification rates could vary because of changes in general legal strategy rather than bankruptcy.

Regression analysis addresses these problems by estimating bankruptcy's impact while holding case and firm characteristics constant. A logistic regression model was used to estimate the odds ratio for bankruptcy's impact on the identification rate. The odds of an event are

$$\frac{p}{1-p},$$

where p is the probability of an event occurring. The odds ratio is the ratio of the odds of an event under one set of circumstances to the odds under another set of circumstances. In this case, the odds ratio is the ratio of the odds that a firm's products are identified postbankruptcy to the odds that the firm's products are identified prebankruptcy. An odds ratio less than 1 indicates a decline in the odds that a firm's products are identified postbankruptcy relative to the odds that they are identified prebankruptcy. To control for case and firm characteristics, we included two sets of indicator variables in the logistic regression—one for the case and one for the firm.[2]

---

[2] That is, the logistic regression includes a set of case fixed effects and a set of firm fixed effects. The variable on the left side in the logistic regression is an indicator variable (a variable taking on the value of 0 or 1) that is 1 if exposure to the firm's product is indicated and 0 otherwise. The logistic regression was estimated using the logistic command in the Stata software package.

Plaintiff's occupation is presumably an important determinant of the types of asbestos-containing products to which the plaintiff was exposed, but it is not included in the regression analysis. We did not use data on plaintiff's occupation in part because the data on primary occupation provided by the large claim servicer with which we worked were often missing for the plaintiffs in our sample and because a plaintiff's occupation can change during the course of a career. But even if occupation were available, it could not be used in a regression with fixed case effects—a categorical variable describing occupation is perfectly correlated with the fixed effects.

To capture what appears to be a gradual response of litigants to bankruptcy, odds ratios are estimated for three periods following bankruptcy:

- the first year following bankruptcy
- the second year following bankruptcy
- two or more years following bankruptcy.

For each of the three periods, the odds ratio compares the odds that a firm's products are identified in cases filed during the period and the odds that they are identified in cases filed prior to bankruptcy.

As can be seen from the first row of Table 3.2, the odds ratios when the case is filed within one year of bankruptcy are not statistically different from 1, indicating that we cannot reject the hypothesis that bankruptcy has no effect on the probability that a firm's product will be identified in interrogatories during the first year following bankruptcy. However, the odds ratio drops considerably once more time has elapsed since bankruptcy. For the BNS cases, the odds ratios declines to 0.306 for cases filed between one and two years after bankruptcy and to 0.168 for cases filed two or more years postbankruptcy. The odds ratio for the WCN cases declines less precipitously for the WCN cases, but the declines are still substantial.[3] Recall from Chapter Two that the WCN cases are represented by a set of plaintiffs' firms that is entirely different from those in the BNS cases.

The odds ratios for cases filed two or more years postbankruptcy are statistically different from 1.0. However, the standard errors reported in Table 3.2 do not consider correlation in the error term of the logistic regression caused by multiple case–firm combinations for the same case and for the same firm. The effect of potential cor-

---

[3] The identification rate considers exposure to be indicated when a claim has been submitted to the firm's bankruptcy trust. As discussed in footnote 10 in Chapter Two, some argue that not all trust claims should be included in an analysis of bankruptcy's effect on product identification. We thus reran the analysis when submission of a trust claim is not considered to indicate exposure to the trust's products. The results were very similar to those in Table 3.2. For the BNS cases, the odds ratios were 0.631, 0.313, and 0.204, with similar statistical significance levels. The results for the WCN cases were unchanged because none of the interrogatories coded for those cases indicated that a trust claim had been submitted.

Table 3.2
Logistic Regression Analysis of Bankruptcy's Effect on Product Identification in Interrogatories (for 43 firms that filed for bankruptcy between 1998 and 2010)

	BNS Cases[a]		WCN Cases[b]	
Case–Firm Combination	Odds Ratio	95% Confidence Interval[c]	Odds Ratio	95% Confidence Interval
Case filed within one year of bankruptcy	0.785	0.281, 2.193	1.096	0.307, 3.910
Case filed from one to two years after bankruptcy	0.306**	0.105, 0.895	0.444	0.119, 1.665
Case filed two years or more after bankruptcy	0.168***	0.061, 0.463	0.264**	0.071, 0.989

NOTE: We have omitted from the table coefficients for the constant term and case and firm fixed effects.

[a] We input 1,634 case–firm combinations into the logistic regression. We ran the logistic regression on the 874 combinations that remained after combinations dropped for which there was no variation in product identification within a case or within a defendant. For the BNS cases, we dropped five firms and 15 cases.

[b] We input 1,634 case–firm combinations into the logistic regression. We ran the logistic regression on the 667 combinations that remained after combinations dropped for which there was no variation in product identification within a case or within a defendant. For the WCN cases, we dropped 14 firms and 15 cases.

[c] The true underlying odds ratio falls within this range with 95-percent probability.

** The odds ratio is statistically different from 1.0 at the 5-percent significance level.

*** The odds ratio is statistically different from 1.0 at the 1-percent significance level.

relation was evaluated in a linear regression framework. As shown in Appendix B, once error correlations are considered, the declines remain statistically significant for BNS case–firm combinations for which the case was filed two years or more postbankruptcy. The declines are still of considerable magnitude but no longer statistically significant for the WCN cases when the error correlations are considered. A conclusion that bankruptcy reduces the odds that the products of bankrupt parties are identified WCN cases should thus be viewed as tentative. A larger sample of cases would increase the precision of the estimates.

The same approach was used to estimate bankruptcy's average effect across the two sets of cases. As shown in Appendix B, the average bankruptcy effects across the two sites are similar to those calculated separately for the BNS and WCN cases. Because of the larger sample size, the standard errors of the estimates decline and the statistical significance of the results improves. As a result, the average effects for cases filed between one and two years postbankruptcy and two or more years postbankruptcy are both statistically significant even when error correlations are considered.

Odds ratios sometimes, but not always, closely approximate the relative risk of two different states (in this case, the identification rate post- versus prebankruptcy).[4] Table 3.3 provides examples of what the odds ratios from the logistic regressions imply for the identification rate. If we use the tabulations in Table 3.1, the prebankruptcy rate is set at 20 percent and the postbankruptcy identification rates calculated from the odds ratio. The odds ratios estimated for the BNS cases imply that a prebankruptcy identification rate of 20 percent would fall to very low levels—4 percent—for cases filed two years or more after bankruptcy. If we use the prebankruptcy rate for the WCN cases in Table 3.1 (10 percent), the identification rate for cases filed two or more years postbankruptcy would fall to 3 percent.

Table 3.3
Illustration of Change in Product-Identification Rates Postbankruptcy

Measure	BNS Cases	WCN Cases
Odds ratio	0.168	0.264
Assumed identification rate prebankruptcy	20	10
Projected identification rate two years postbankruptcy	4	3
95% confidence interval on identification rate two years postbankruptcy	1, 10	1, 10

---

[4]   Odds ratios and relative risk will be similar when the initial probability is low and the odds ratio is not far from 1 (Huw Talfryn Oakley Davies, Iain Kinloch Crombie, and Manouche Tavakoli, "When Can Odds Ratios Mislead?" *British Medical Journal*, Vol. 31, No. 6, 1998, pp. 989–991).

There is a variety of plausible explanations for a gradual (as opposed to immediate) fall in the identification rate postbankruptcy. For example, a gradual response could result from ongoing personnel turnover at the major plaintiffs' firms. The attorneys handling a case filed shortly after a new bankruptcy will likely have handled cases prior to the bankruptcy and be familiar with the products of the newly bankrupt firm. Given this familiarity, they might continue to identify the bankrupt party in similar cases (which implies that they do not narrowly respond to disincentives to identify the bankrupt firm's products). Over time, however, new, younger attorneys come into the firm who might have no knowledge about the bankrupt party. The party is no longer named on the complaint, and the new attorneys have no reason to inquire into exposures to these firms' products.[5] The result would be a gradual decline in identification rate as the cumulative turnover grows. A second potential explanation for gradual decline is hedging by plaintiffs' attorneys on whether the bankruptcy will be approved. When a firm files for bankruptcy, an automatic stay takes effect immediately that shields the firm from suit. But a bankruptcy judge must review and confirm the bankruptcy filing—a process that can take several years. It is possible that the bankruptcy will be denied and no trust set up for asbestos claims. Plaintiffs' attorneys could conceivably want to wait until more information is available about the likely outcome of the bankruptcy case before changing identification practices.

The results in Table 3.2 fall between the findings in the Garlock bankruptcy case and those in Scarcella, Kelso, and Cagnoli (2012). Recall from the discussion of the Garlock opinion in Chapter One that the plaintiffs identified approximately 10 percent of the bankrupt parties to which they were exposed. The findings in Scarcella, Kelso,

---

[5] Using the same methodology as used for interrogatories and depositions, we also examined bankruptcy's impact on the parties named in complaints. As expected, the identification rate drops to very low levels during the first year following bankruptcy and remains at low levels thereafter.

and Cagnoli (2012) translate to roughly 50 percent.[6] The scenarios in Table 3.3 imply that between 20 and 30 percent of firms that would have been identified prebankruptcy would be identified once two or more years have elapsed since bankruptcy.[7] It should be noted, however, that the statistical confidence intervals for the postbankruptcy identification-rate projections (see bottom row of Table 3.3) are fairly wide and include percentages that would produce the 10-percent finding in the Garlock case and the 50-percent finding from the Scarcella, Kelso, and Cagnoli (2012) study.[8]

Findings When We Include the Products Identified in Depositions

So far, our analysis has considered only the products identified in interrogatory answers. If the number of products identified in interrogatories falls after bankruptcy, one might expect additional products to be identified during the depositions. In this section, we consider bankruptcy's impact on the products identified when we consider both interrogatories and depositions.

As expected, adding depositions to the analysis increases the product-identification rate for the 43 firms examined. Table 3.4

---

[6] Scarcella, Kelso, and Cagnoli (2012) found that, on average, approximately eight defendants that eventually filed for bankruptcy were identified in the prebankruptcy period versus four in the postbankruptcy period (see discussion in Chapter One).

[7] According to the BNS figures in Table 3.3, 20 percent of firms that go bankrupt would be identified prebankruptcy, and 4 percent of the same firms would be identified postbankruptcy. This implies that 20 percent ($0.04 \div 0.20$) of firms to whose products the plaintiff was exposed would be identified postbankruptcy. This result for the WCN cases is 30 percent ($0.03 \div 0.10$).

[8] For the BNS cases, a postbankruptcy rate would need to be 2 percent to match the 10-percent finding in the Garlock case—and 2 percent falls in the 95-percent confidence interval for the projections here. For the WCN cases, the postbankruptcy rate would need to be 1 percent—which is the lower bound of the 95-percent confidence interval found here. The postbankruptcy rates would have to be 10 percent and 5 percent for the BNS and WCN cases, respectively, to match the Scarcella, Kelso, and Cagnoli (2012) findings—and these rates are also in the 95-percent confidence intervals.

Table 3.4
Product-Identification Rate Pre- and Postbankruptcy for Cases with Both Interrogatories and Depositions

Case–Firm Combination	BNS Cases[a]		WCN Cases[b]	
	Identification Rate (%)	N	Identification Rate (%)	N
Case filed prebankruptcy				
Interrogatory only	12	333	8	403
Interrogatory and deposition	16	333	13	403
Case filed postbankruptcy				
Interrogatory only	11	484	4	887
Interrogatory and deposition	13	484	8	887

NOTE: We omitted from the table coefficients for the constant term and case and firm fixed effects. N refers to the number of case–firm combinations.

[a] The results for the BNS cases are based on the 19 cases for which both interrogatories and depositions were obtained (817 case–firm combinations, representing 19 cases times 43 firms).

[b] The results for the WCN cases are based on the 30 cases for which both interrogatories and depositions were obtained (1,290 case–firm combinations, representing 30 cases times 43 firms).

reports identification rates pre- and postbankruptcy for those cases for which we could obtain both interrogatories and depositions. The product-identification rate prebankruptcy increases from 12 to 16 percent for the BNS cases once depositions are added. Postbankruptcy, the product-identification rate for the BNS cases increases from 11 to 13 percent. Similar increases are observed for the WCN cases.

Although including depositions increases the product-identification rate, bankruptcy still appears to have a negative impact on the product-identification rate when we consider both interrogatories and depositions. For example, the product-identification rate for BNS cases falls from 16 percent prebankruptcy to 13 percent postbankruptcy.

Bankruptcy's impact on product identification controlling for case and firm characteristics is reported in Table 3.5. Including the products identified in depositions does not qualitatively change the results obtained when only interrogatories are considered. Again, the odds ratio falls considerably as the time between case filing and bankruptcy increases, and the declines are large. The odds ratios are statistically different from 1.0 for cases filed two years or more postbankruptcy. When we combine the two sets of cases to estimate an average

Table 3.5
Logistic Regression Analysis of Bankruptcy's Effects on Product Identification in Interrogatories and Depositions (for 43 firms that filed for bankruptcy between 1998 and 2010)

	BNS Cases[a]		WCN Cases[b]	
Case–Firm Combination	Odds Ratio	95% Confidence Interval[c]	Odds Ratio	95% Confidence Interval
Case filed within one year of bankruptcy	0.267**	0.081, 0.879	0.879	0.223, 3.465
Case filed from one to two years after bankruptcy	0.154***	0.040, 0.589	0.794	0.209, 3.01
Case filed two years or more after bankruptcy	0.091***	0.023, 0.358	0.303*	0.074, 1.23

NOTE: We base this analysis on those cases with depositions—regardless of whether an interrogatory was obtained.

[a] We input 1,204 case–firm combinations into the logistic regression (28 cases times 43 firms). We ran the logistic regression on the 496 combinations that remained after combinations dropped for which there was no variation in product identification within a case or within a defendant.

[b] We input 1,333 case–firm combinations into the logistic regression (31 cases times 43 firms). We ran the logistic regression on the 728 combinations that remained after combinations dropped for which there was no variation in product identification within a case or within a defendant.

[c] The true underlying odds ratio falls within this range with 95-percent probability.

* The odds ratio is statistically different from 1.0 at the 10-percent significance level.

** The odds ratio is statistically different from 1.0 at the 5-percent significance level.

*** The odds ratio is statistically different from 1.0 at the 1-percent significance level.

bankruptcy effect across the two sites, the statistical significance of the results rises (see Appendix B).

To provide some insight into efforts that defendants are making to elicit exposure to the products of bankrupt parties, Table 3.6 tallies the different types of product-identification responses recorded in the documents. To more clearly understand what the depositions add, we restrict the tabulations to cases with both interrogatories and depositions. The rows labeled "exposure affirmed" repeat figures from the second and fourth rows of Table 3.4, showing the percentage of case–firm combinations in which exposure was affirmed. The "don't know or unsure" rows show the rate at which plaintiffs said they did not know or were unsure whether they were exposed to products of each of the 43 firms included in the analysis. And the "exposure denied"

Table 3.6
Product-Identification Responses in Interrogatories and Depositions for Cases with Both Interrogatories and Depositions

	BNS Cases		WCN Cases	
Response Type	Percentage of Case–Firm Combinations	N	Percentage of Case–Firm Combinations	N
Case filed prebankruptcy				
Exposure affirmed	16	333	13	403
Don't know or unsure	0.6	333	8	403
Exposure denied	0.3	333	5	403
Any mention of the firm	16	333	19	403
Case filed postbankruptcy				
Exposure affirmed	13	484	8	887
Don't know or unsure	0	484	3	887
Exposure denied	0.6	484	2	887
Any mention of the firm	13	484	11	887

NOTE: N refers to number of case–firm combinations.

rows show the rate at which plaintiffs explicitly denied that they were exposed to the firm's products. The percentage of case–firm combinations in which the firm was mentioned in any way in the interrogatories and depositions is reported in the remaining row of the table.[9]

The results indicate that defendants in the BNS cases, both pre- and postbankruptcy, rarely asked about exposures to the products of one of the 43 firms analyzed here and that plaintiffs rarely denied or responded that they did not know or were unsure about the exposure. The frequencies for "don't know or unsure" and "exposure denied" are considerably higher for the WCN cases; however, in both sets of cases, there is little indication that it is more common for defendants to ask postbankruptcy about exposures that plaintiffs then deny or respond that they do not know or are unsure about them. Combined with the findings that the product-identification rate falls postbankruptcy, the findings in Table 3.6 suggest that, during depositions, defendants do little to counter the decline in the number of firms identified in interrogatories by exploring exposures to bankrupt parties not identified in interrogatories. As we discuss in the next chapter, there are several possible explanations for defendants choosing not to pursue these exposures during deposition.

---

[9]   Because the different depositions of the same party might conflict or the depositions of different parties might conflict, the percentage of case–firm combinations for which a firm was mentioned might be less than the sum of the other three categories.

CHAPTER FOUR

Discussion

The extent to which exposures to the asbestos-containing products of bankrupt firms are identified during a tort case has important implications for plaintiffs and remaining solvent defendants. The failure of plaintiffs and defendants to identify all such exposures can mean that a remaining solvent defendant will pay more than it would if all exposure were identified. Failure to identify exposure to the products of bankrupt parties might also result in greater plaintiff compensation than otherwise from bankruptcy trusts and the tort case combined. As discussed in Chapter One, plaintiffs thus have disincentives to identify exposure to bankrupt firms' products, while defendants have incentives to do so.

Our analysis provides evidence that bankruptcy does change plaintiff behavior in asbestos cases brought in New York. We found similar results for cases brought in California, although the results are more tentative because of the greater statistical imprecision of the estimates. The results suggest that, in the year following bankruptcy, the probability that a firm's product is identified in interrogatories (which are completed by the plaintiffs' attorney or paraprofessional) does not change a great deal but that it drops substantially in following years. Once two or more years has passed since bankruptcy, a firm is substantially less likely to be identified than it would have if the same case had been filed prior to the firm's bankruptcy. Our analysis also suggests that defendants do little in the deposition phase of the case to counter the drop in identification rates by exploring exposures to bankrupt parties not identified in interrogatories.

Our findings are based on cases brought in two states by plaintiffs with particular types of exposure histories. These results cannot automatically be extrapolated to other states with different liability regimes, to states with different requirements for showing that exposure contributes to injury, and to other exposure histories in which maritime law does not apply.

We shared interim findings with plaintiffs' attorneys, defendants, and defense attorneys, and the two sides had very different perspectives on what the findings mean and whether the findings are a cause for concern. From the prospective of most plaintiffs' attorneys with whom we spoke or who provided written comments, the findings were not a problem. Some noted that it is appropriate for plaintiffs to focus on the solvent defendants that remain in the case and that, from the plaintiffs' perspective, there would be no reason to proactively identify other sources of exposure.

Some plaintiffs' attorneys further noted that defendants have ample opportunity under the rules of civil procedure to explore exposure to products of bankrupt firms—for example, during depositions—if they choose to do so. Plaintiffs' attorneys also noted that defendants can use a variety of other approaches to introduce exposure evidence besides through interrogatories and depositions: They can call experts during trial, they can introduce ship logs and other information on work history to establish exposure, and they can also typically introduce into evidence depositions and interrogatories from other cases with similar plaintiffs. Plaintiffs' attorneys point out that, even though this study shows a drop in product identification based on interrogatories and depositions, all exposures might end up being identified if the case proceeds all the way to verdict. If a case settles before verdict, those settlements are voluntary on the defense's part.

The defendants and defense attorneys with whom we spoke have a very different perspective. They believe that case-management orders require plaintiffs and their lawyers to identify all exposures to asbestos-containing products in pretrial discovery, not just the products of those companies they are pursing in litigation. Defendants argue that it is very difficult to establish exposure to an asbestos-containing material absent a plaintiff's statement (or coworker's or family member's) to that effect. The reason is that asbestos-containing products can vary throughout a jobsite, as can the types of tasks performed, so simply establishing that the plaintiff worked at a particular site might not be enough to establish exposure to a bankrupt party's products.[1] They explain that, even though a defendant can hire experts to prove that a plaintiff was exposed to the product of a bankrupt party, doing so is much more expensive and less persuasive than a plaintiff's acknowledgment of exposure to such products. In their experience, defendants are often better off paying higher settlements than paying the costs of litigating around missing exposure evidence. Consequently, this study's finding that the product-identification rate falls postbankruptcy is of major concern to defendants.

Defendants identify a variety of factors that discourage them for probing exposure to a bankrupt party's product during deposition. For example, judges often impose time limits on depositions, and, given the large number of defendants involved in most cases, there might be time to cover only exposures to the products of the parties currently active in the case. There also might be little return in asking plaintiffs to detail exposure to products of bankrupt parties; furthermore, by asking, defendants open themselves up to the possibility that the plaintiff will deny exposure, which will make it more difficult to establish exposure based on other sources later on. Some defendants also worry that plaintiffs' attorneys will retaliate if they pursue additional exposures too aggressively by confronting them with even more claims by plaintiffs who recall exposure to their products but not to those of bankrupt parties. They are also concerned that juries might not be able to distinguish their products from similar products of bankrupt firms, so establishing exposure to bankrupt parties' products might only increase their liability. For these reasons, defendants conclude

---

[1] For discussion of causation requirements in asbestos cases, see S. Todd Brown, "Bankruptcy Trusts, Transparency and the Future of Asbestos Compensation," *Widener Law Journal*, Vol. 23, No. 1, 2013, p. 309: To establish specific causation with respect to a defendant, the plaintiffs must proceed by "acknowledging exposure to [the defendant's] products and putting forward witnesses who attested to personal knowledge of the plaintiffs' presence when those products were used."

that plaintiffs' failure to identify exposures in interrogatories postbankruptcy is a significant problem.

Not only is there substantial disagreement on whether the postbankruptcy decline in product identification is a problem; there is also a divergence of views on what, if anything, should be done about it. Defendants argue for extending and better enforcing requirements that trust claims be filed before trial.[2] They argue for greater transparency regarding the claims submitted to bankruptcy trusts and the basis for payment.[3] They support modifying case-management orders so that it is absolutely clear that plaintiffs should disclose all exposures to asbestos-containing products in interrogatory responses, regardless of whether a product was produced by a currently bankrupt firm. Plaintiffs' lawyers typically do not support such changes. Current procedure, they contend, provides ample opportunity for each side to put on its best case.[4]

This study has collected empirical evidence of how bankruptcy affects litigant behavior in terms of product identification. We hope that the findings will inform the debate over whether and what type of reform is desirable.

---

[2]   There is currently no requirement in California regarding when a trust claim must be filed during a court case. A case-management order in New York City requires plaintiffs to file all trust claims before trial in certain asbestos cases, but there are indications that compliance with the order is uneven (Dixon and McGovern, 2011, pp. 62, 68–69). It is worthy of note, however, that a recent case-management order entered by the judge managing the asbestos docket in Los Angeles requires plaintiffs

> to disclose all facts relating to all of their alleged exposures to asbestos, whether . . . to bankrupt or other entities, and regardless of whether those facts have been, or ever will be, included in a claim to a third party for the purpose of obtaining compensation for an asbestos-related injury. (*In re Los Angeles Asbestos Litigation*, "Case Management Order Requiring Disclosure of Bankruptcy Trust Claims, Claims-Related Materials, and Asbestos Exposure Facts," Super. Ct. Calif., April 7, 2015, p. 2)

[3]   For example, the Furthering Asbestos Claim Transparency Act would require bankruptcy trusts to provide quarterly the name and exposure history of each claimant and the basis for any payment made to such claimant (U.S. House of Representatives, Furthering Asbestos Claim Transparency Act of 2013, H.R. 982, passed the House amended November 13, 2013).

[4]   For further discussion of potential legislative and procedural reforms, see Vairo, 2014, pp. 1050–1070.

Firms Whose Product Identification We Analyzed

Table A.1 lists alphabetically the firms included in the analysis. In addition to the primary name, we list the divisions, subsidiaries, and otherwise-related firms that plaintiffs called out in the complaints,

Table A.1
Firms Whose Product Identification We Analyzed

Primary Name	Bankruptcy Date	Division or Subsidiary Grouped Under Primary Name
ABB Lummus	April 21, 2006	—
A. C. and S.	September 16, 2002	—
A. P. Green Industries	February 14, 2002	A. P. Green Refractories A. P. Green Services Bigelow-Liptak Corporation General Refractories Company
Armstrong World Industries	December 6, 2000	Armstrong Cork and Seal Armstrong Cork Company
ARTRA	June 3, 2002	Synkoloid Company
Babcock and Wilcox Company	February 22, 2000	B and W Refractories Limited
Bondex International	May 31, 2010	RPM International
Burns and Roe Enterprises	December 4, 2000	—
C. E. Thurston and Sons	August 18, 2003	—
Combustion Engineering	February 17, 2003	Heine Boiler Company Refractory and Insulation

Table A.1—Continued

Primary Name	Bankruptcy Date	Division or Subsidiary Grouped Under Primary Name
Congoleum Corporation	December 1, 2003	American Biltrite Amtico Congoleum-Nairn
Dana Corporation	March 3, 2006	Spicer Corporation
Dresser Industries	February 14, 2002	Dresser-Rand Company Global Industrial Technologies Harbison-Walker Refractories Company M. W. Kellog Company Worthington Corporation Worthington Pump and Machinery Company Worthington Turbine
Durabala Manufacturing Company	April 12, 2010	—
E. J. Bartells Company	October 20, 2000	—
Federal Mogul	October 1, 2001	Fel-Pro Ferodo Flexitallic Gasket Holdings Turner and Newall T and N Industries Wagner Electric Corporation
Flintkote Company	May 1, 2004	—
Fuller Austin Insulation	September 4, 1998	—
G-1 Holdings	May 5, 2001	GAF Corporation Ruberoid
Garlock	June 6, 2010	Anchor Packing Company EnPro Industries Fairbanks Morse Engine Fairbanks Morse Pump Corporation Fairbanks Valves Garlock Sealing Technologies Quincy Compressor Company

Table A.1—Continued

Primary Name	Bankruptcy Date	Division or Subsidiary Grouped Under Primary Name
General Motors Corporation	June 1, 2009	Delphi Corporation Delphi Harrison Thermal Systems Harrison Radiator
Hercules Chemical Company	September 18, 2008	—
J. T. Thorpe and Son	February 12, 2002	J. T. Thorpe
Lake Asbestos of Quebec	August 9, 2005	ASARCO Incorporated Capco Pipe Company Lac D'Amante Du Quebec
Leslie Controls	July 12, 2010	—
M. H. Detrick Company	January 13, 1998	—
North American Refractories Company	January 4, 2002	Allied Signal Bendix Corporation Honeywell International
Owens-Corning Fiberglass Company	October 5, 2000	Fenco Corporation Fibreboard Corporation Fibreboard Paper Products Corporation Pabco
Pittsburgh Corning Corporation	April 16, 2000	—
Plant Insulation	March 13, 2009	—
Plibrico Company	March 13, 2002	Plibrico Refractories
Porter Hayden Company	March 15, 2002	—
Quigley Company	September 3, 2004	Pfizer
Rock Wool Manufacturing	November 18, 1995	—
Rutland Fire and Clay Company	October 13, 1999	—
Shook and Fletcher	April 8, 2002	—
Skinner Engine Company	April 16, 2001	—
Stone and Webster Engineering Company	June 2, 2000	—

Table A.1—Continued

Primary Name	Bankruptcy Date	Division or Subsidiary Grouped Under Primary Name
T. H. Agriculture and Nutrition Company	November 24, 2008	Elementis Chemicals Philips Electronics
U.S. Gypsum Company	June 25, 2001	—
U.S. Mineral Products Company	June 23, 2001	—
Western MacArthur Company	November 22, 2002	Bay Cities Asbestos Company MacArthur Company Western Asbestos Company
W. R. Grace and Company	April 1, 2001	—

interrogatories, and depositions.[1] We grouped these firms with the primary name in the analysis. Doing so avoids situations in which the disappearance of a firm name is taken to signal that the firm's products are no longer identified by the plaintiff when, in fact, the firm has been subsumed into another firm and the product in question is being indirectly referenced under a different name. We took efforts to identify these interrelationships to protect against the possibility that an overly narrow definition of a firm would exaggerate bankruptcy's effects on product identification.

---

[1]   Note that the table does not provide a listing of all divisions and subsidiaries of the primary company. It lists only those that appeared in the documents reviewed.

Alternative Approaches for Estimating Bankruptcy's Effect on Product Identification

The logistic regression analysis described earlier did not consider the possibility of correlation in the error term caused by repeated observations for the same case or the same firm. In this appendix, we first reestimate the statistical models in a linear regression framework, which allows for consideration of error clustering. We then estimate the average bankruptcy effect across the two sets of cases.

Corrections for Error Correlations

Table B.1 presents results for our analysis of bankruptcy's effects on product identification in interrogatories (corresponding to the logistic

Table B.1
Linear Regression Analysis of Bankruptcy's Effect on Product Identification in Interrogatories (for 43 firms that filed for bankruptcy between 1998 and 2010)

Case–Firm Combination	Ordinary Least Squares		Cameron, Gelbach, and Miller Estimate	
	Coefficient	Standard Error	Coefficient	Standard Error
BNS case[a]				
Case filed within one year of bankruptcy	−0.026	0.055	−0.026	0.080
Case filed from one to two years after bankruptcy	−0.140**	0.058	−0.140*	0.075

Table B.1—Continued

Case–Firm Combination	Ordinary Least Squares		Cameron, Gelbach, and Miller Estimate	
	Coefficient	Standard Error	Coefficient	Standard Error
Case filed two years or more after bankruptcy	−0.219***	0.056	−0.219**	0.097
WCN case[b]				
Case filed within one year of bankruptcy	−0.027	0.069	−0.027	0.059
Case filed from one to two years after bankruptcy	−0.083	0.066	−0.083	0.096
Case filed two years or more after bankruptcy	−0.139**	0.067	−0.139	0.107
BNS or WCN case (BNS and WCN cases combined)[c]				
Case filed within one year of bankruptcy	−0.036	0.036	−0.036	0.049
Case filed from one to two years after bankruptcy	−0.118***	0.036	−0.118**	0.050
Case filed two years or more after bankruptcy	−0.208***	0.035	−0.208***	0.075

NOTE: We omitted from the table coefficients for the constant term and case and firm fixed effects.

[a] Same observations used as in logistic regression reported in Table 3.2 in Chapter Three (N = 874 case–firm combinations). Adjusted R-squared = 0.398.

[b] Same observations used as in logistic regression reported in Table 3.2 in Chapter Three (N = 667 case–firm combinations). Adjusted R-squared = 0.202.

[c] Same observations used as in logistic regression reported in Table B.2 (N = 1,932 case–firm combinations). Adjusted R-squared = 0.333.

* The coefficient statistically differs from 0 at the 10-percent significance level.

** The coefficient statistically differs from 0 at the 5-percent significance level.

*** The coefficient statistically differs from 0 at the 1-percent significance level.

regression results in Table 3.2 in Chapter Three). The second and third columns report results from the ordinary-least-squares regressions run on the same set of observations used in the estimates of the logistic regressions reported in Table 3.2. The last two columns report results corrected for two-way clustering in the error term. The correction is done using the CGMREG routine written for Stata by A. Colin Cameron at the University of California, Davis.[1] The regression coefficients reflect the change in the probability that a firm's products are identified postbankruptcy relative to the probability that they are identified prebankruptcy (a coefficient of −0.2, would indicate a drop from 0.40, for example, to 0.2 [on a scale of 0 to 1.0]). Consistently with the results from the logistic regression, the bankruptcy effects manifest gradually over time, and the changes when cases are filed one to two years and two years or more after bankruptcy are statistically different from 0. As expected, the coefficients remain the same once the error correlations are considered, but the standard errors of the coefficients increase. The coefficients remain statistically different from 0 but at a lower significance level. The results for the BNS cases suggest that a statistically significant relationship between bankruptcy and product identification remains once we consider the error correlations.

Bankruptcy's effect on product identification in interrogatories is not as large for the WCN cases, but, as before, the effect increases as the time since bankruptcy grows. Once we consider the error correlations, none of the coefficients is statistically different from 0 at the 10-percent significance level. Thus, the findings for the WCN should be viewed as tentative.

Average Bankruptcy Effect Across Both Sets of Cases

To calculate bankruptcy's average effect across the two sets of cases, the two sets of cases are combined and a site indicator variable is added to the regression model. The results for the logistical regression based on interrogatories only are presented in the top half of Table B.2, and the corrections for error correlation are reported in the last set of rows in

---

[1] For a description of the method, see A. Colin Cameron, Jonah B. Gelbach, and Douglas L. Miller, "Robust Inference with Multiway Clustering," *Journal of Business and Economic Statistics*, Vol. 29, No. 2, 2011, pp. 238–249. The code for calculating the corrected standard errors is available at A. Colin Cameron, "cameron_miller_JHR_files to share.zip," archive, July 8, 2014.

Table B.2
Logistic Regression Analysis of Bankruptcy's Average Effect on Product
Identification (for 43 firms that filed for bankruptcy between 1998 and
2010)

	BNS and WCN Cases Combined	
Case–Firm Combination	Odds Ratio	95% Confidence Interval
Interrogatory only[a]		
Case filed within one year of bankruptcy	0.778	0.389, 1.558
Case filed from one to two years after bankruptcy	0.323***	0.156, 0.669
Case filed two years or more after bankruptcy	0.163***	0.081, 0.332
Site indicator variable (WCN cases set to 1)	1.493	0.473, 4.710
Interrogatory and deposition[b]		
Case filed within one year of bankruptcy	0.413**	0.181, 0.943
Case filed from one to two years after bankruptcy	0.299***	0.127, 0.705
Case filed two years or more after bankruptcy	0.111***	0.046, 0.266
Site indicator variable (WCN cases set to 1)	4.230	1.196, 14.962

NOTE: We omitted from the table coefficients for the constant term and case and
firm fixed effects.

[a] We input 3,268 case–firm combinations into the logistic regression (76 cases
times 43 firms). We ran the logistic regression on the 1,932 combinations that
remained after combinations dropped for which there was no variation in product
identification within a case or within a defendant.

[b] We input 2,107 case–firm combinations into the logistic regression (49 cases
times 43 firms). We ran the logistic regression on the 1,596 combinations that
remained after combinations dropped for which there was no variation in product
identification within a case or within a defendant.

** The odds ratio is statistically different from 1.0 at the 5-percent significance level.

*** The odds ratio is statistically different from 1.0 at the 1-percent significance
level.

Table B.1. The average bankruptcy effects across the two sites are similar to those calculated separately for the BNS and WCN cases. Because
of the larger sample size, the standard errors have declined and the statistical significance of the results has improved. In the bottom half of

Table B.2, we present the average effect when we consider both inter-rogatories and depositions. These are the average effects correspond-ing the separate regressions for the two sites reported in Table 3.5 in Chapter Three.

References

Brown, S. Todd, "Bankruptcy Trusts, Transparency and the Future of Asbestos Compensation," *Widener Law Journal*, Vol. 23, No. 1, 2013, pp. 299–375.

Cameron, A. Colin, "cameron_miller_JHR_files to share.zip," archive, July 8, 2014. As of March 25, 2015:
http://cameron.econ.ucdavis.edu/research/
cameron_miller_JHR_files%20to%20share.zip

Cameron, A. Colin, Jonah B. Gelbach, and Douglas L. Miller, "Robust Inference with Multiway Clustering," *Journal of Business and Economic Statistics*, Vol. 29, No. 2, 2011, pp. 238–249.

Carroll, Stephen J., Deborah R. Hensler, Jennifer Gross, Elizabeth M. Sloss, Matthias Schonlau, Allan Abrahamse, and J. Scott Ashwood, *Asbestos Litigation*, Santa Monica, Calif.: RAND Corporation, MG-162-ICJ, 2005. As of March 24, 2015:
http://www.rand.org/pubs/monographs/MG162.html

Crowell and Moring, "Chart 1: Company Name and Year of Bankruptcy Filing (Chronologically)," 2660535, revised September 19, 2014. As of March 24, 2015:
http://www.crowell.com/files/
List-of-Asbestos-Bankruptcy-Cases-Chronological-Order.pdf

Davies, Huw Talfryn Oakley, Iain Kinloch Crombie, and Manouche Tavakoli, "When Can Odds Ratios Mislead?" *British Medical Journal*, Vol. 31, No. 6, 1998, pp. 989–991.

Dixon, Lloyd, and Geoffrey McGovern, *Asbestos Bankruptcy Trusts and Tort Compensation*, Santa Monica, Calif.: RAND Corporation, MG-1104-ICJ, 2011. As of March 24, 2015:
http://www.rand.org/pubs/monographs/MG1104.html

Dixon, Lloyd, Geoffrey McGovern, and Amy Coombe, *Asbestos Bankruptcy Trusts: An Overview of Trust Structure and Activity with Detailed Reports on the Largest Trusts*, Santa Monica, Calif.: RAND Corporation, TR-872-ICJ, 2010. As of March 24, 2015:
http://www.rand.org/pubs/technical_reports/TR872.html

In re Complex Asbestos Litig., "Defendants' Standard Interrogatories to Plaintiff (Personal Injury) [Set One]," Super. Ct. California, County of San Francisco, Case CGC-84-828684, November 26, 2013. As of March 25, 2015:
http://www.sfsuperiorcourt.org/sites/default/files/images/
Case%20Management%20Oorder%20Feb%202014.pdf

In re Garlock Sealing Techs., LLC, 2014 Bankr. LEXIS 155, January 10, 2014.

In re Los Angeles Asbestos Litigation, "Case Management Order Requiring Disclosure of Bankruptcy Trust Claims, Claims-Related Materials, and Asbestos Exposure Facts," Super. Ct. Calif., April 7, 2015.

In re: New York City Asbestos Litigation, "Defendants' Third Amended Standard Set of Interrogatories and Request for Production of Documents," Appendix C, N.Y. 2001.

Lindstrom v. A-C Prod. Liab. Trust, 424 F.3d 488 (6th Cir.), September 28, 2005.

"Mesothelioma: Malignant," *MedlinePlus*, updated May 29, 2014. As of March 24, 2015:
http://www.nlm.nih.gov/medlineplus/ency/article/000115.htm

Peck, Robert S., "The Development of the Law of Joint and Several Liability," *Federation of Defense and Corporate Counsel Quarterly*, Vol. 55, No. 4, Summer 2005, pp. 469–478.

Scarcella, Marc C., and Peter R. Kelso, "Asbestos Bankruptcy Trusts: A 2013 Overview of Trust Assets, Compensation and Governance," *Mealey's Asbestos Bankruptcy Report*, Vol. 12, No. 11, June 2013, pp. 33–47.

Scarcella, Marc C., Peter R. Kelso, and Joseph Cagnoli, Jr., "The Philadelphia Story: Asbestos Litigation, Bankruptcy Trusts and Changes in Exposure Allegations from 1991–2010," *Mealey's Litigation Report: Asbestos*, Vol. 27, No. 17, October 10, 2012, pp. 1–13.

U.S. Code, Title 11, Bankruptcy, Chapter 5, Creditors, the debtor, and the estate, Subchapter II, Debtor's duties and benefits, Section 524, Effect of discharge. As of March 24, 2015:
http://www.gpo.gov/fdsys/granule/USCODE-2011-title11/
USCODE-2011-title11-chap5-subchapII-sec524

U.S. House of Representatives, Furthering Asbestos Claim Transparency Act of 2013, H.R. 982, passed the House amended November 13, 2013. As of March 25, 2015:
https://www.congress.gov/bill/113th-congress/house-bill/982

Vairo, Georgene, "Lessons Learned by the Reporter: Is Disaggregation the Answer to the Asbestos Mess?" *Tulane Law Review*, Vol. 88, No. 6, 2014, pp. 1039–1070.